nature's friends

Fish

by Ann Heinrichs

Content Adviser: Dr. Barry Chernoff, Curator of Fishes, The Field Museum of Natural History, Chicago, Illinois

Science Adviser: Terrence E. Young Jr., M.Ed., M.L.S., Jefferson Parish (La.) Public Schools

Reading Adviser: Dr. Linda D. Labbo, Department of Reading Education, College of Education, The University of Georgia

COMPASS POINT BOOKS
MINNEAPOLIS, MINNESOTA

Compass Point Books
3109 West 50th Street, #115
Minneapolis, MN 55410

Visit Compass Point Books on the Internet at *www.compasspointbooks.com*
or e-mail your request to *custserv@compasspointbooks.com*

Photographs ©: Dave B. Fleetham/Visuals Unlimited, cover, 1; Tom Brakefield/Corbis, 4–5; Dave Haas/The Image Finders, 6–7, 8–9; David Wrobel/Visuals Unlimited, 10–11; Dwight R. Kuhn, 12–13, 18–19; Wernher Krutein/photovault.com, 14–15; DigitalVision, 16–17; David B. Fleetham/Tom Stack & Associates, 20–21; Tom & Therisa Stack/Tom Stack & Associates, 20–23; Humann/gtphoto, 24; John M. Roberts/Corbis, 26–27.

Editors: E. Russell Primm, Emily J. Dolbear, Pam Rosenberg, and Patricia Stockland
Photo Researcher: Svetlana Zhurkina
Photo Selector: Linda S. Koutris
Designer: The Design Lab

Library of Congress Cataloging-in-Publication Data
Heinrichs, Ann.
  Fish / by Ann Heinrichs.
      p. cm. — (Nature's friends)
  Summary: Introduces physical characteristics, methods of movement, habitats, feeding habits, life cycles, and different types of fish.
  Includes bibliographical references (p.   ).
  ISBN 0-7565-0435-X (hardcover)
  1. Fishes—Juvenile literature. [1. Fishes.] I. Title.
  QL617.2 .H45 2003
  597—dc21   2002009934

Table of Contents

*NOTE: In this book, words that are defined in the glossary are in **bold** the first time they appear in the text.*

What Is a Fish?

You know what a fish looks like. You can probably draw a nice one. Some fish don't look like fish at all, however. Flatfish are flat like pancakes. Eels are long like snakes. Even seahorses are really fish. What makes them all fish?

Fish are cold-blooded animals. That doesn't mean their blood is cold. It means their bodies stay the same temperature as the water they live in.

Fish breathe **oxygen** underwater with **gills.** Dolphins and whales are not fish. They are mammals like us. They breathe with lungs.

All fish are vertebrates. This means they have backbones. Jellyfish and starfish are not really fish. They have no backbones or spinal cords.

Fish are able to breathe underwater because they have gills.

A Fish's Body

Have you ever seen a goldfish? Most fish have the same kind of shape. They have **fins** to help them swim.

The bodies of most fish are covered with scales. Scales protect fish from sickness, cuts, and scratches. Many fish have gills that are like sharp hooks. These help protect them against **predators.**

A fish has two round eyes. Most fish have jaws, teeth, and a tongue. Jaw teeth may be used to catch food. A fish has special throat teeth for chewing.

Gills are on each side of the head. To breathe, a fish gulps water. Then the water passes through the gills. The gills remove oxygen from the water.

A fish has a heart. It pumps blood through the body. The stomach and intestines digest food.

Fish use fins to help them swim. ▶

How Do Fish Know Things?

Fish can see, smell, hear, taste, and feel. They can do some extra things, too.

Fish smell through their nostrils. Salmon use their sense of smell to find the streams where they were born. They travel back to their birthplace to lay their eggs!

Fish have ears, but you cannot see them. Their ears are inside their skulls.

Fish have a system called the lateral line. The lateral line helps the fish feel movements in the water. Tiny hairs in this system can feel **vibrations.** This helps fish swim in schools, avoid predators, and find food. The lateral line tells them how near or far an object is. This is helpful in dark water.

◀ *This school of fish can sense each other's vibrations.*

Kinds of Fish

There are more than twenty thousand species of fish. They come in all sizes. Gobies are only three-quarters of an inch (2 centimeters) long. Whale sharks are more than 60 feet (18 meters) long!

Most fish have skeletons made of bones. Most bony fish have rayed fins. These are the fins you probably think of when you think of fish. These fins are spiny and spread out like a fan. Some bony fish have lobe fins. These fins are fleshy and **floppy.**

Some fish have cartilage skeletons. Cartilage is a tough material that bends. Sharks and rays have cartilage skeletons.

Some fish have no jaws. They have a round mouth for sucking food. Lampreys have no jaws. Some lampreys feed on other fish. They hang on to a fish with their mouth and suck from its body.

Some fish, such as this cabezon, have spiny fins. ▶

Why Don't Fish Sink?

Throw a baseball into the water. It sinks. Many fish are heavier than baseballs, however. Why don't they sink?

Most fish have swim bladders. The swim bladder is right under the backbone. It fills with gases. A full bladder helps the fish float.

What if the fish wants to swim deeper? That's easy. In deeper water, the swim bladder gets smaller. It fills up again as the fish swims upward. By using their swim bladders, fish are able to stay at any depth.

Sharks and rays have no swim bladders. They have to keep swimming. If they don't, they sink. Some sharks and rays have large livers that are filled with oil. These livers make the sharks and rays more **buoyant.** This helps them float.

◀ *A swim bladder allows this betta to swim at any depth.*

Where Fish Live

Fish live just about everywhere there is water. They live in icy waters or hot springs. Some live in high mountain streams. Others live at the bottoms of the seas and oceans.

Marine or saltwater fish live in the ocean. Many of them stay near a coast. They find food and shelter there. Freshwater fish live in waters surrounded by land. They live in lakes, rivers, ponds, or caves.

Lungfish live where there's not much rain. Their water home dries up. The lungfish bury themselves in the mud and curl up into a ball. They secrete **mucus,** which hardens to form a cocoon. They live curled up in the cocoon until the next rainfall. Months may pass before it rains. Then they live as fish again.

A lungfish ▶

What Fish Eat

Most fish eat other animals. That includes insects, worms, shrimp—and fish. Most fish eat plants. They like algae and other water plants.

Some fish eat plankton. Plankton are microscopic animals and plants.

Fish have many ways to get food. Swordfish have long, pointy beaks. They catch fish by waving their bills from side to side. This movement cuts up the fish. Then they pick up the wounded prey and eat it. Archerfish see insects flying in the air. They spit water at the insects to knock them into the water. Then they can easily suck up the insects.

◂ Sharks eat other fish.

Laying Eggs and Growing Up

Most fish reproduce in **spawning grounds.** These places are where they were born. Some travel thousands of miles to get back there.

Most female fish lay eggs. Some lay millions of eggs at once! Then the male releases sperm on them. The sperm fertilize the eggs so they can develop.

Some fish make a nest for their eggs. Some guard their young after they hatch. Fish that do care for their young are usually males. Females usually lay their eggs and leave.

A newly hatched fish is called a larva. Most larvae don't look like their parents. They may have huge bellies and eyes. They go through changes as they grow. When they can reproduce, they are adults.

Newly hatched spined stickleback larvae (center) do not look like adult fish. ▶

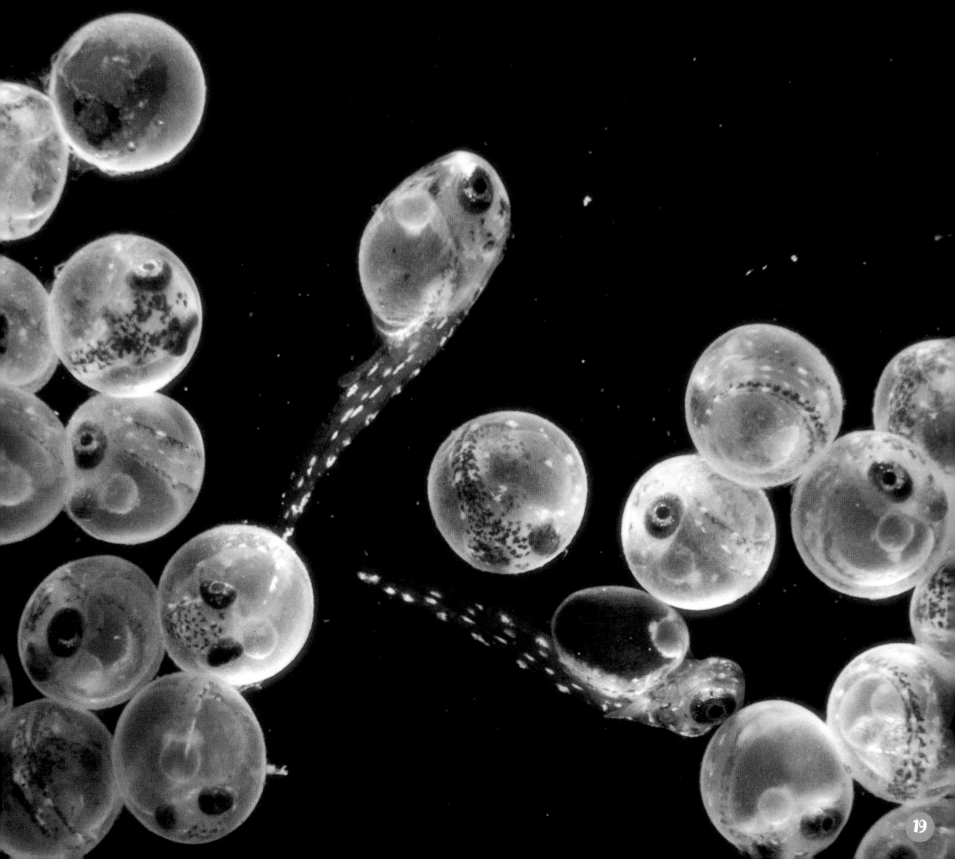

Keeping Safe

Fish must stay out of danger. They could be eaten at any minute! Luckily, they have many ways to keep safe.

A fish's color often matches where it lives. This is called camouflage. It blends in with rocks, plants, or water. Some fish look like something else. Stonefish look like stones. Leafy sea dragons look like seaweed.

Most fish have scales to protect their skin. Some have sharp spines. These sharp points make them hard to swallow. Some spiny fish contain poison. Some nonpoisonous fish copy the colors of poisonous fish. This helps keep predators away.

Flying fish fly from danger. They leap into the air. They stretch out their big fins like wings. Then they **glide** through the air and use their tails to keep moving.

This leafy sea dragon tricks enemies by looking like seaweed.

Living Together

How many children are in your school? Let's say you are a herring. Then your answer would be "millions"!

Some fish swim around in schools, or big groups. They stay safe and find food together.

Some fish are called cleaners. They live very closely with other fish called hosts. The host is a welcome visitor. The cleaner eats tiny animals off the host's body. It's as if the two fish made a deal. "You clean me, and I'll feed you."

There are even some fish that depend on other creatures for protection. One example is the anemonefish. It is sheltered by **sea anemones.** The sea anemones' stinging tentacles protect the anemonefish from its predators. These tentacles don't sting the anemonefish, however.

A school of colorful yellowtail snappers ▶

Weird Fish

Why did the catfish cross the road? To get to another pond! "Walking catfish" can move across land. They travel to reach a new home. They do this when their original home dries up or after a heavy rainfall. They push with their tails and flop forward. Their stiff front fins hold them up.

Some fish light up. The light may attract fish to eat or scare enemies away. The light patterns also attract mates. Some fish produce electricity. They stun or kill their enemies or prey.

Flatfish go through a weird change. A baby flatfish starts life with an eye on each side of its head. As it grows up, one eye moves to the other side of its head. Then both eyes are on the same side. From then on, the flatfish lives on its side!

The white patches underneath this flashlight fish's eyes light up like a flashlight!

Fish Are Good Friends!

Fish are important to the world. They eat smaller plants and animals. Then other animals eat fish. Without fish, nature would be all mixed up. There would be too many of some things. Many other things would die.

Fish are good for people to eat, too. People around the world get protein from fish. Protein helps the body grow and heal. Some fish have material that's made into medicines.

Fish make good pets. Their bright colors are awesome. It's also fun to watch how they live.

Some kinds of fish are dying out. Dirty water kills them, or people drain their waters away. Sometimes people catch too many of them for food. Let's hope our fish friends stay healthy and safe!

Fish help people in many ways.
Some, like these oranda fish, make excellent pets. ▶

Glossary

buoyant—able to keep afloat

fins—parts of a fish's body that look like flaps and help the fish move through water

floppy—soft and able to bend easily

gills—the parts of a fish's body that are used for breathing

glide—to coast or float

mucus—a slippery fluid that coats and protects a body part

oxygen—a gas that is found in air

predators—animals that hunt for other animals and eat them

sea anemones—hollow-bodied sea animals with tentacles that look like flowers clustered around their mouths

spawning grounds—places where water animals lay their eggs

vibrations—very fast back-and-forth movements

Let's Look at the Redbellied Piranha

Class: Actinopterygii
Order: Characiformes
Family: Characidae
Genus: Pygocentrus
Species: nattereri
Range: Found in freshwater river systems in South America

Life span: In the wilds, unknown but at least five years; in aquariums they have survived to at least twenty-five years!

Life stages: The females attach their eggs to the roots of floating plants, particularly those of the water hyacinth. The males then fertilize the attached eggs.

Food: Adult redbellied piranhas are carnivores, or meat eaters. They also eat small amounts of plants and fruits. They usually eat other fish but will eat the flesh of other animals when it is available. Young redbellied piranhas eat the fin rays and scales of other fish.

Did You Know?

Electric fish, especially those from South America, see with their electricity.

Some fish in streams or small rivers can "smell danger." A fish in trouble sends off chemicals. Other fish smell those chemicals. Then they swim away for safety.

Some fish can move back and forth between salt water and freshwater. Most of these fish live in estuaries, which are places where a river meets the sea.

The black swallower can eat fish up to twice its own size. It has hinged jaws that can open very wide. The stomach of the black swallower stretches to make room for the larger fish. It can expand to several times its normal size.

Some fish have large spots that look like eyes on their tail or rear fins. These eyespots can trick predators into attacking the fish's tail instead of its head. Then the fish has a better chance of escaping because it is swimming away from the predator's mouth.

Junior Ichthyologists

Ichthyologists are scientists who study fish. You can be an ichthyologist, too! Try this simple experiment. You will need brine shrimp, boiled spinach, a notebook, a pen or pencil, and a fish tank with at least two goldfish. Before starting this experiment, make sure that you will be able to keep the goldfish as pets. Or make sure you know someone who will give them a home in their aquarium when you are done. Make a chart with two columns in your notebook. Label one column "Brine Shrimp" and the other column "Boiled Spinach." Place some brine shrimp in the water on one end of the fish tank. Place some boiled spinach in the water in the other end of the fish tank. Watch the goldfish. Make a mark in the shrimp column each time one of the goldfish feeds on the brine shrimp. Make a mark in the spinach column each time one of the goldfish feeds on the boiled spinach. Continue watching the fish for fifteen minutes. When you have finished watching the fish, remove any remaining brine shrimp and boiled spinach from the tank.

After watching the fish for fifteen minutes, try to answer these questions:

How many times did the fish feed on the brine shrimp?

How many times did the fish feed on the boiled spinach?

Do you think goldfish prefer to eat brine shrimp or boiled spinach?

If they liked one kind of food better than the other, why do you think it was the favorite?

Draw a picture of a goldfish.

Want to Know More?

AT THE LIBRARY

Earle, Sylvia A., and Wolcott Henry (photographer). *Hello, Fish!: Visiting the Coral Reef.* Washington, D.C.: National Geographic Society, 2001.

Frost, Helen. *Fish.* Mankato, Minn.: Pebble Books, 2001.

Sill, Cathryn P., and John Sill (illustrator). *About Fish: A Guide for Children.* Atlanta: Peachtree Publishers, 2002.

ON THE WEB

Fish Eye View Camera
http://www.fisheyeview.com/
To see live underwater video of fish

Fish Information
http://ncfisheries.net/kids/fish.htm
To learn more about fish and fishing

How Fish Swim
http://www.flmnh.ufl.edu/fish/Education/HowSwim/HowSwim.html
To learn more about how fish swim

THROUGH THE MAIL

National Fish and Wildlife Foundation
1120 Connecticut Avenue, N.W.
Suite 900
Washington, DC 20036
202/857-0166

ON THE ROAD

John G. Shedd Aquarium
1200 South Lake Shore Drive
Chicago, IL 60605
312/939-8069
To see thousands of species of fish from around the world

Steinhart Aquarium
California Academy of Sciences
55 Concourse Drive
Golden Gate Park
San Francisco, CA 94118
415/750-7145
To see the Touch Tide Pool exhibit and fish from many other environments

Index

About the Author: Ann Heinrichs grew up in Fort Smith, Arkansas. She began playing the piano at age three and thought she would grow up to be a pianist. Instead, she became a writer. Now she has written more than eighty books for children and young adults. Several of her books have won national awards. Ms. Heinrichs now lives in Chicago, Illinois. She enjoys martial arts and traveling to faraway countries.